The Musings of a BiPolar Computer Scientist

Rebecca Shepherd

Presentation by *BookLeaf Publishing*

Web: www.bookleafpub.com

E-mail: info@bookleafpub.com

ISBN: 9789357696975

First edition 2022

DEDICATION

To everyone whose mind gets too full. We may
not have a pensieve but we have writing.

ACKNOWLEDGEMENT

To Elaine who took the time to give me feedback, I am so grateful to have you on my side.

To my best friend who read all my poems, despite not liking poetry, I love you.

To my family who have been my amazing support system, I couldn't have done any of this without you.

And finally, to my amazing fiancé who supports me and loves me not matter what, there are not enough poems in the world to illustrate my love for you.

PREFACE

I just wrote exactly how I was feeling or what I was thinking. It's probably pretty random but hopefully that means that, if you're reading this, something will resonate with you. I hope you enjoy it but even if you don't, I just appreciate your time.

Change

As much as society has moved forward,
It feels as though some things will never change.
People say they believe in change.
Institutions say they support change.
Everybody says they want change.

Until something happens.
A comment, a word, a tweet.
And you realise, really, there has been no change at all.
Except they change in your eyes.
And you change.

You withdraw, you make different decisions.
Decisions about where you go,
Who you spend time with,
What classes you take.
And suddenly you've changed.

But society will move forward, right?
Things will get better, right?
People will learn, right?
Right?
Meanwhile, all you can do is keep going.

Hope for change for the future,
Hope for change for your children,
And hope you don't change too much whilst you wait.

Different

They say everyone is different,
And that being different is a 'good' thing.
Isn't it?
Until it isn't, I guess.

Because people do like different,
So long as it's their kind of different.
They like different in a way they understand,
That suits them.

But what if you are different?
Different in a way they can't,
Or won't understand?
What happens then?

Well then being different isn't so 'good'.
Then being different becomes difficult.
Because people don't really want different.
They just want a variation instead.

Fracture

Have you ever heard of a stress fracture?
Typically found in the foot.
It's a fracture due to repetitive force.
Repetitive force.

But this fracture is hard to see.
Even with an x-ray or scans.
It's painful and swells and lasts a long time.
Lasts a long time.

The only thing to do is rest,
And wait, for it takes time to fully heal.
And people are okay because: fracture!
Because it's a fracture.

Well, I have fractured my spirit,
Fractured from repetitive force.
When it's not a bone they tell you push through.
They tell you, push through.

And so, you do, you apply more force,
And the fracture becomes a break.
And suddenly your crazy, weird, or broken.
Crazy, weird, broken.

So, rest, and ignore what the others say.
Rest because you need it.
Rest because you deserve it.
Rest before you break.
Rest Before you break.

Joy

In a lot of ways, I am so lucky.
And one of those ways is that I get to see joy.
True, unadulterated joy.

I see joy when a bride walks in,
And they see the white, the sparkles, the beauty.

I see joy on their mother's face,
That they get to be a part of this special moment.

I see joy when the nerves wash away,
And she sees her true beauty, maybe for the first time.

I see joy when she looks in the mirror,
And realises, she is a bride.

I see joy when I put a veil on her head
And everyone, even me, starts to tear up.

I am so incredibly lucky.
Because I don't just see joy.
I cause joy.
I share their joy.
And I will be forever grateful for that joy.

Names

I have been called Drama Queen.
I have been called Annoying.
I have been called Emotional.
I have been called Loud.

I have been called Depressed.
I have been called Anxious.
I have been called Bipolar.
I have been called Borderline.

I have been called Liar.
I have been called Fake.
I have been called Attention Seeker.
I have been called Unlikeable.

Some of these things I am.
Most of these things I am not.
But realistically, the only thing I should be called,
Is Human.

Rules

I live my life surrounded by rules.
The rules of society.
The rules set by me.
The rules of writing code.
The rules I write in code.
Rules, Rules, Rules.

And as a rule, I like rules.
They keep me balanced.
They keep me sane.
They keep me on track.
They stop my code from breaking.
Except, Except, Except.

Except when those rules don't work.
What then?
Except when society's rules contradict your own.
What then?
Except when the rules feel wrong.
What then?

Well then you have to ignore the rules.
Or bend the rules.
Or break the rules.
Or make new rules.
Basically, despite all these rules, we're just winging it.
And hoping we're flying the right way.

Taboo

Being a woman is not easy.
That doesn't mean, being you isn't hard.
But being a woman is NOT easy.

Did you know?
Because I didn't know.
Because there are things that no one tells you.

Because we don't talk about those things.
So, you believe there's something wrong with you.
That you are the problem.
When in fact, you just weren't told.

You weren't told what's normal.
You weren't told that it's different from the movies and the
books.
Because, somehow, you were supposed to know.

So let's start talking.
Let's tell each other.
Let's lift the taboo.

Because you didn't know.
And that's okay.
It is okay not to know.

Because I can tell you.
And you can tell me.
And together we can learn.
Because it is time we tell.

Age

Age is just a number,
At least that's how the saying goes.
But age is as much a feeling,
As a number that always grows.

You feel your age around children,
Who are just beginning to grow.
You feel your age around students,
Who have so much they don't know.

But then you see your parents,
And it's their age you start to feel.
Because you see them growing old,
And mortality becomes all too real.

So age isn't just number, and it's okay to feel.
Because age is a part of life, and death, and
unfortunately, that's the deal.

Expectations

People always had high expectations of me,
And often those 'people' included myself.
I scored highly on tests, took part in clubs,
I was supposed to go far, that is until my health.

You see I had signs as a child,
Signs I wouldn't let the world see.
So when I could no longer hide these signs,
People changed their expectations of me.

Now I have to fight to be heard,
And people don't always believe.
Because those signs are out there now,
And people think all they do is deceive.

But I am still me and I am still smart.
Just because my brain works differently, doesn't
mean I can't tell the difference between my head and
my heart.

Family

My family and I are close,
We're very lucky that way.
We talk over skype every week,
And I call my parents to tell them about my day.

We all live far apart,
On different sides of the country.
But we all put our lives aside,
And meet up on a Monday.

Sometimes we do a quiz,
Or watch a movie or just sit and chat.
It's never anything big,
But it forces us to relax and sit back.

I know not everyone's family is as close as mine,
But if you have someone you love, trust me, it's
worth taking the time.

Geek

I am a geek,
I am as stereotypical as it gets.
With asthma and allergies and glasses.
And the social anxiety stress.

But I love being a nerd,
Or a geek or whatever you want to call me.
Because I get to love so many things,
And there's a strong sense of community.

Communities with people who love the same shows as you,
Communities with people who read the same books.
Communities with people who will play games with you,
And communities with people who go to conventions and
dress up.

We geeks are weird and wonderful and beautiful,
Because we are all so different but will still support you.

Love Part 1

I have found my love,
And I know that sounds kind of gross.
We're taught that being mushy is weak,
And not to get too close.

And yet we listen to love songs,
And poems by the bard.
So, I'm going to tell you about my love,
And I'm going to let down my guard.

Because my love feels like glasses,
Like seeing for the first time.
He makes things clear and easy,
And I still can't believe he's mine.

There's more that I can say, so I won't stop here.
Turn over to continue, because this you want to hear.

Love Part 2

Thank God for online dating,
Because without it, we would have never met.
As an adult it can be hard to meet people,
So you need to change your mindset.

And he really changed my mindset.
In more ways than one.
He made me more patient, and kind,
And he helps me have more fun.

He calms my anxieties,
And supports my mental health.
He has this calming bubble,
And he's always just, himself.

So don't be afraid of soppy, I guess I'm trying to say.
Because you will find someone at some point that
you could write poetry about all day.

Magic

We all need a little bit of magic,
And it can come from anywhere.
But sometimes you need to make your own magic,
Because, sometimes, life just isn't fair.

I find magic in the change of seasons,
And in writing with a quill.
But I sometimes lose the magic,
And sometimes, I lose the will.

But then something just happens,
And it's usually something small.
But you have to be open to the magic of it,
Or it won't change anything at all.

So be open to the magic, and try to look everywhere,
Because I promise you, not matter what, there is
always magic there.

Manic

There are times when you will see me happy.
I will be bubbly and loud and outgoing.
But sometimes the happy you see is not happy,
And from the outside there is no way of knowing.

You can't know that inside I'm screaming,
And banging on an internal glass wall.
Because I'm shouting that it isn't real,
And I have no control over it at all.

And then I will go home,
And the anxiety will set in.
Because, despite my best efforts, I wasn't myself,
And it's depressing when you just can't win.

So try to be patient, and try to understand,
Because I know it can be annoying, but I'm doing
the best I can.

Opportunity

Some say that crime is opportunity,
What better opportunity than war?
Someone took opportunity of me,
Then left me, alone, to die on the floor.

They took me from my home, or us I should say.
They saw us and stole us to use for their own gain.
In us they found me, and they took me away.
They smashed me, and broke me, and left me in pain.

They wanted what they couldn't have from me,
But they forced it out of me anyway.
They took my golden centre that you can't see.
They took my heart and left me where I lay.

So, who am I? This mysterious 'her'
I am, in fact, the Golden Lyre of Ur.

Path

I thought I knew what I wanted,
And I chased it as hard as I could.
But then I didn't get it,
And realised that I had misunderstood.

Because what I wanted, wasn't right.
Or at least not right for me.
It wasn't what I needed.
It wasn't what I was meant to be.

So, I needed to rethink,
And try to find my place.
When suddenly it came to me.
And my old path was replaced.

And now I know that this path, is right.
And I will finish this path, be it day, or night.

Reader

I have been a Shadowhunter,
And fought alongside Jace and Clary.
I have gone to Hogwarts,
And been on adventures with Ron, Hermione, and Harry.

I have lived in Morganville,
And been a part of the glass house.
I have followed the Baudelaire orphans,
And been inspired by Sunny, Violet, and Klaus.

I have fallen in love with a werewolf,
A vampire and a fairy too.
I have volunteered, and been chosen,
And proven my heart to be true.

Life can be really hard, and it can leave you shook,
But I am a reader, and I get to live in the land of books.

Soulmate

I have a great romantic love,
But I have a soulmate as well.
My soulmate is my best friend,
And she has seen me through hell.

She is wonderful, and talented,
And she never ceases to amaze.
She is so much more than my best friend,
And I will love her until the end of my days.

I know when she's upset,
Even though she's far away.
She likes to call me the oracle,
Because I predicted her first kiss down to the day.

We both have found great romantic loves, but we talk
all the time.
Because she is my soulmate, my best friend, my
partner in crime.

Thank You

I just wanted to say Thank You.
If you've got this far.
Because it means you've read my poetry,
And in my eyes, that makes you a star.

I hope it wasn't too terrible,
And maybe it made you feel.
But even if it didn't,
I promise, everything I've said is real.

And if you didn't like it,
I promise that's okay.
Because I just appreciate your time,
And being a part of your day.

So I can't say it enough but thank you thank you
thank you,
Because you just made me smile, and because of
you I grew.

WISTEM

I am a woman in STEM,
Which I like to shorten to WISTEM.
Because it sounds like I'm making a wish,
And it also sounds like wisdom.

STEM stands for Science, Technology, Engineering and
Mathematics,
In case you didn't know.
And getting more women in these subjects,
Is still a wish because society moves slow.

But there are those of us out there,
Fighting to be heard.
Fighting against sexist lecturers and students,
Which at this point is absurd.

So, I am part of WISTEM and I say that loud and proud,
Because this kind of inequality, shouldn't still be allowed.